Duck (widgeon)

Canada goose

Mute swan

Ducks are smaller than geese
and spend more time on water.

They have shorter necks than geese.

Male and female geese
look very much alike.

Male and female ducks
are usually different in colour.

The male bird is called the drake.

He usually has brighter colours.

The females have duller colours.

THE "READ ABOUT IT" SERIES

BOOK 108

DUCKS, GEESE AND SWANS

by

O. B. GREGORY

Illustrated by Elsie Wrigley

WHEATON

A Member of the Pergamon Group

08 017174 5

DUCKS, GEESE AND SWANS

Ducks, geese and swans
    all belong to the same family.

They are all water birds
    but sometimes they feed on land.

They are all quite big birds.

The swans are the biggest.

The ducks are the smallest.

Duck (teal)

Drake

Some ducks feed on the
surface of the water.

The mallard, teal and shoveler
are surface feeders.

Some ducks dive for their food.

The tufted duck, pochard, goldeneye
and eider are diving ducks.

Many ducks stay in Britain
all the year round.

The long-tailed duck
and the goldeneye
are winter visitors.

Teal

Mallard

Shoveler

Tufted duck

Eider

Pochard

The picture shows a pair of mallards
   with their young.
You can also see a drake feeding.

The drake has a green head
   and a white collar.

The female is brown.

Mallards live on lakes,
   rivers and ponds.

They usually nest among grass
   near to water.

From eight to fourteen eggs are laid.

The mallard is a good flier.

It can take off
   straight from the water.

The teal is a handsome bird.

The drake has a green band
on each side of the head.

The teal is our smallest duck.

The male goldeneye has a white patch
under each eye.

The female's head is dark brown
all over.

The eider duck is a sea bird
except when it is nesting.

The female lines her nest with down
from her own body.

She is brown in colour.

The drake is white and black
with a pink breast.

Teal

Goldeneye

Eider

The picture shows a shelduck.

This is the largest British duck.

It lives near the coast.

It eats worms, shellfish, snails
and seaweed.

Shelducks are rather like geese
in some of their ways.

They spend more time on land.

The male and female birds
are nearly alike in colour.

They fly more like geese,
beating their wings
more slowly than ducks.

The picture shows three more members
of the duck family.

They are the goosander,
the red-breasted merganser
and the smew.

They are sometimes called "sawbills".

Inside their beaks they have
rows of little lumps
like the teeth of a saw.

Sawbills eat fish.

The "teeth" help them to hold
wet, slippery fish.

Goosander

Merganser

Smew

The picture shows a grey lag goose.

It looks something like
a farmyard goose.

They grey lag goose
nests in Scotland.

Since 1969 grey lag geese have
been nesting in England as well.

Most wild geese in Britain
are winter visitors.

They come to us from
Greenland and Iceland.

They keep together in flocks.

They fly in a V formation
or in a wavy line.

Swans are larger than geese
and spend more time on water.

They have longer necks than geese
but shorter legs.

Most grown up swans are white.

The male swan is called the cob.

The female is called the pen.

The young swans are called cygnets.

Swans are heavy birds
and cannot take off at once.

They must first taxi along the water
flapping their wings as they go.

There are three kinds of swan
in Britain.

Two of them are winter visitors
but one stays in Britain
all the time.

This is the mute swan.

The mute swan has an orange beak.

The other swans have yellow beaks.

Swans eat water plants and insects.

They nest on the ground near water.

Swans take great care of their young.

After they have left the nest
the young are carried
on the parent's back.

THINGS TO WRITE

1 What is the male duck called? (4)

2 Name four diving ducks. (6)

3 Which mallard has a green head? (8)

4 Which mallard is brown? (8)

5 Where do mallards nest? (8)

6 Which is our smallest duck? (10)

7 Which bird has a white patch
under the eye? (10)

8 What does the eider duck use
to line her nest? (10)

9 Which is the largest British duck? (12)

10 Where does the shelduck live? (12)

11 What does the shelduck eat? (12)

12 Describe the way shelducks fly. (12)

13 Which birds
    are sometimes called sawbills? (14)

14 What do sawbills eat? (14)

15 Where does the grey lag goose
    nest? (16)

16 What is the male swan called? (18)

17 What is the female swan called? (18)

18 What are young swans called? (18)

19 How do swans take off? (18)

20 Which swan has an orange beak? (20)

VOCABULARY

The running words in this book are taken from the Dale list and the commoner reading schemes, together with the following additional words on the pages indicated. A word in brackets is used elsewhere in this birds series.

p.	2	(geese)	
p.	4	(male)	
		(female)	
		(usually)	
		drake	
		(duller)	
p.	6	(surface)	
		(mallard)	
		teal	
		(shoveler)	
		dive	
		tufted	
		pochard	
		goldeneye	
		eider	
		(diving)	
p.	8	collar	
		fourteen	
		(August)	
p.	10	(patch)	
		(pink)	
		(breast)	

p. 12	shelduck
	(coast)
	(worms)
	(snails)
p. 14	(goosander)
	red-breasted
	merganser
	sawbills
	slippery
p. 16	lag
	(goose)
	(Scotland)
	(Greenland)
	(Iceland)
	(flocks)
	formation
p. 18	cob
	cygnets
	(taxi)
p. 20	(mute)
	(insects)

Printed in Great Britain by A. Wheaton & Co, Exeter